Design Elements 4

A Visual Reference by
Richard Hora
Mies Hora

The Art Direction Book Company, New York

Dedicated to Jil
and to all those who utilize this book.

Book design by Richard and Mies Hora
Special thanks to
Don Barron and David Freedman
for their generous assistance.

Art Direction Book Company
10 East 39th Street
New York, New York 10016

Library of Congress Catalog Card Number 81–66127
International Standard Book Number 0–910158–97–5

Forward

This book is the fourth in a series which
represents many years of collection
and use, beginning as a working tool and
developing into a labor of love. The
material was carefully selected from a wide
variety of sources, both old and new,
and many elements were created specifi-
cally for this volume. The elements are
generously sized for reproduction purposes
and organized into convenient categories.
We hope you find *Design Elements 4*
to be the inspirational and easy-to-use
source file that we intended.

Richard Hora
Mies Hora

Introduction

Sometimes a designer starts with an idea and finds the visual form to express it. Other times the idea is triggered by visual input. The design process is a constant interplay between idea and form, form and idea. This series provides a wealth of imagery with which to express ideas and is also a valuable visual resource from which ideas can grow.

In the first two volumes, the 'elements,' including circles, suns, stars, arrows and hearts, are truly 'elemental.' As we follow the Horas' thorough exploration of these forms from page to page, we are led naturally to an understanding of the forms themselves. The third volume is a compendium of borders and dingbats, designed forms carefully selected for their beauty and utility.

Design Elements 4 is an extension of the previous volumes, with more complex forms, completing this rich collection of images. The quality of the selections is matched by the clarity of presentation and attention to detail.

These books provide a good foundation for graphic designers, and they are a valuable addition to every design library.

David Freedman
Designer
Milton Glaser, Inc.

Contents

Snowflakes
Decorative Motifs:
(quilt)
(radial)
(circular)
(Pennsylvania Dutch)
(Early American)
(square)
Ribbons/Bows

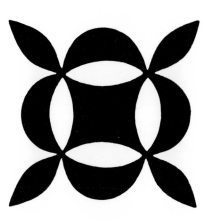
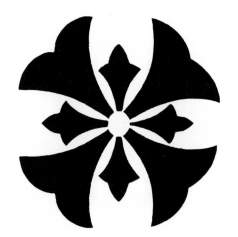
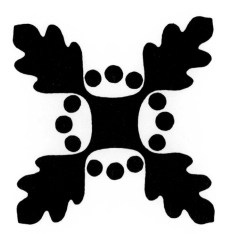

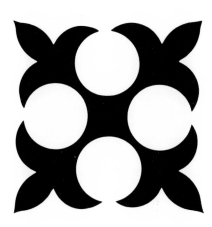

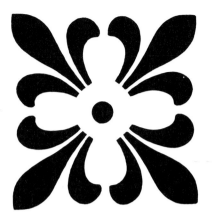

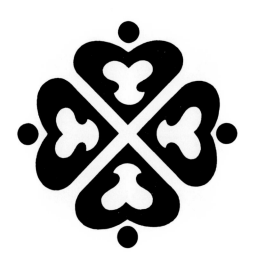

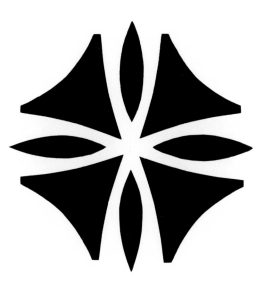

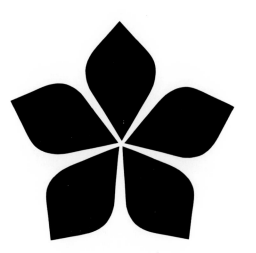

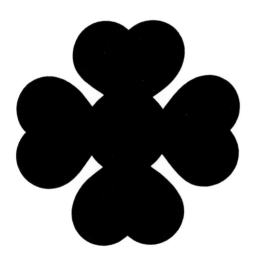

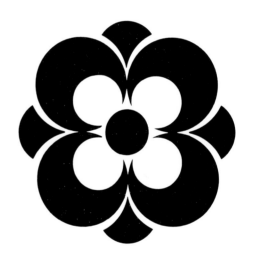

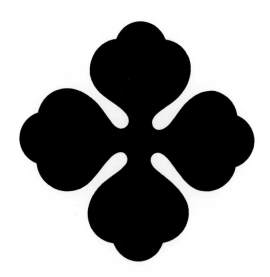

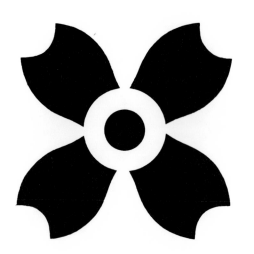

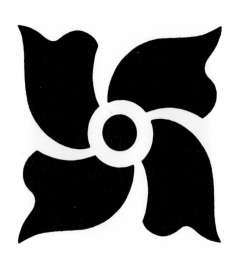

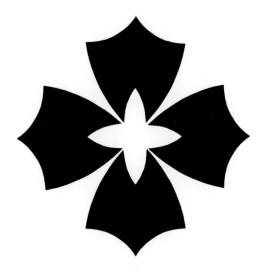

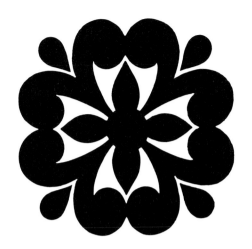

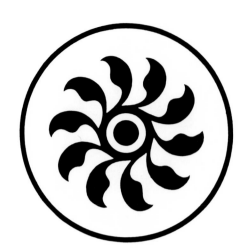

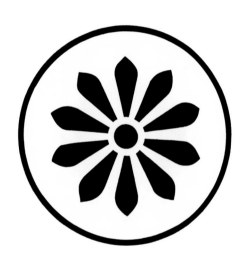

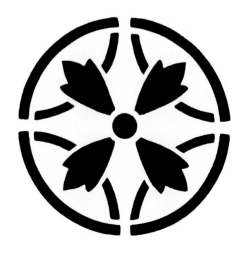

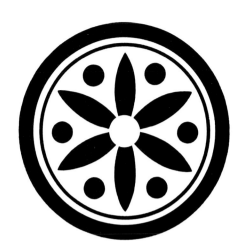

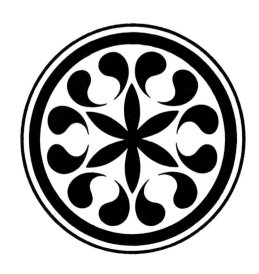

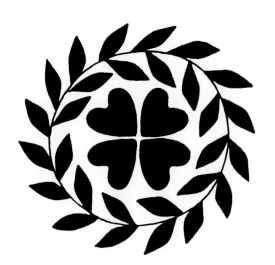

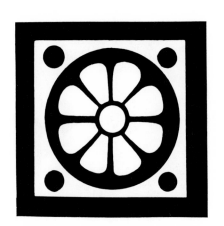

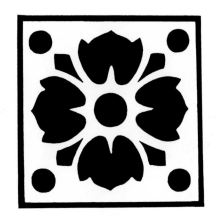

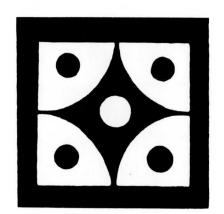

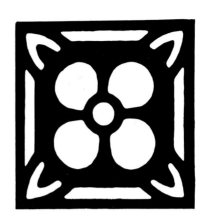

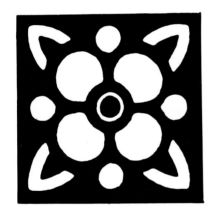

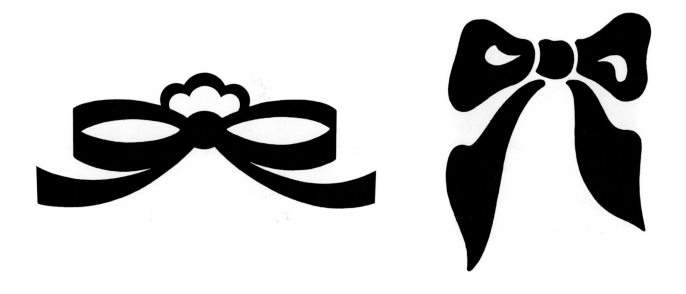

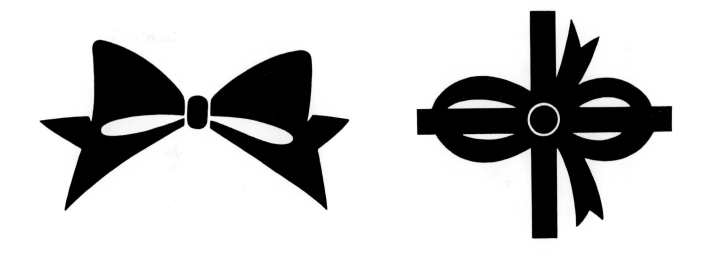

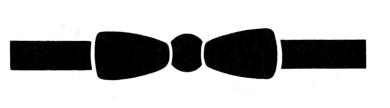

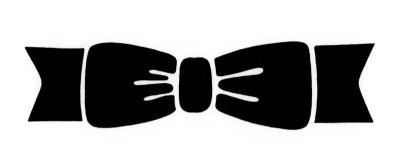

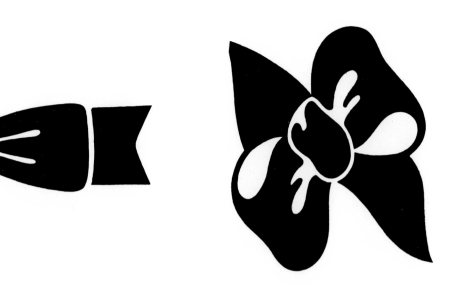

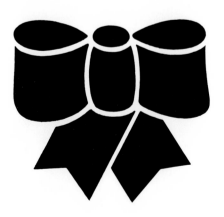

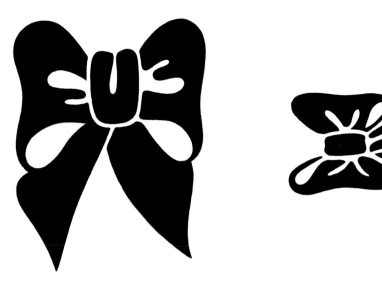

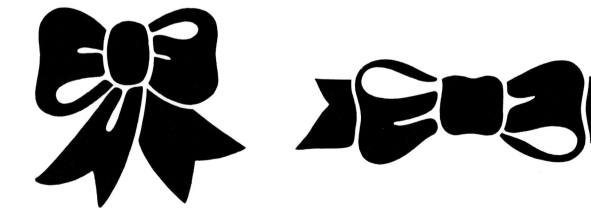

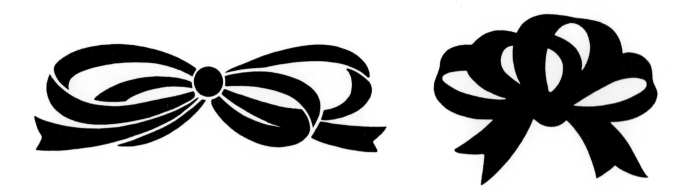

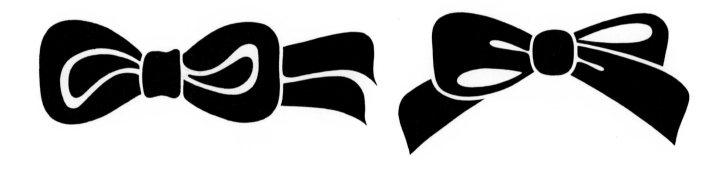

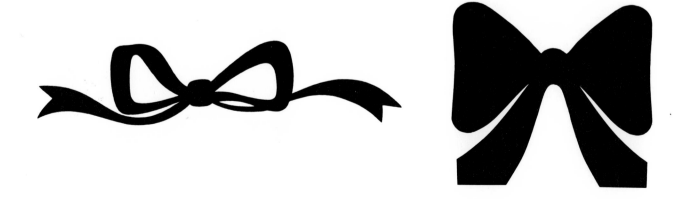

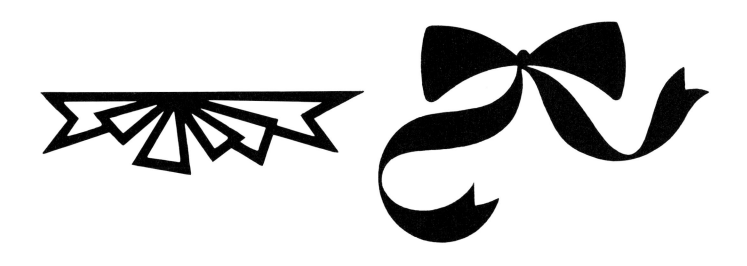

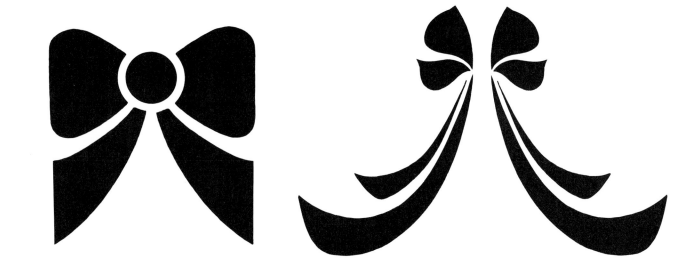

Floral Designs
Floral Designs (holly)
Floral Adornments
Adornments

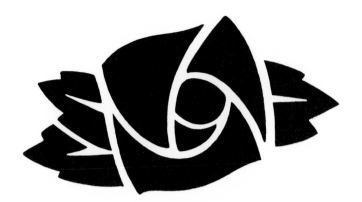

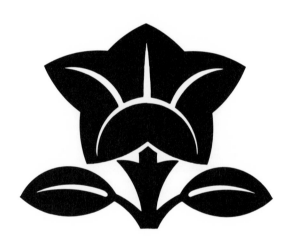

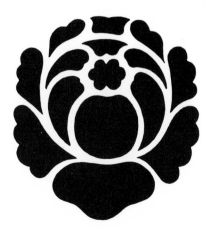

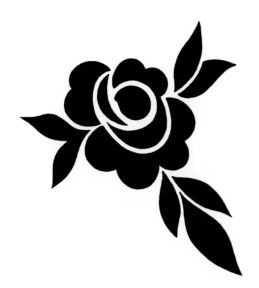

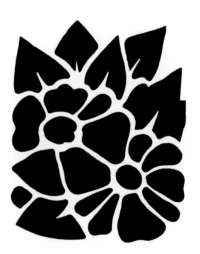

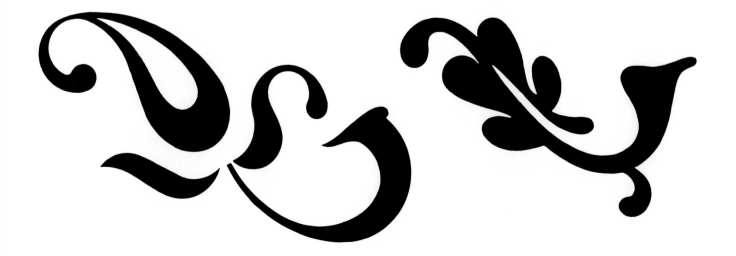

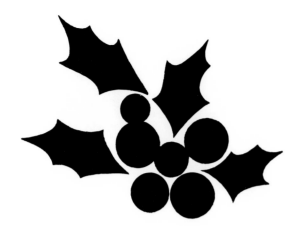
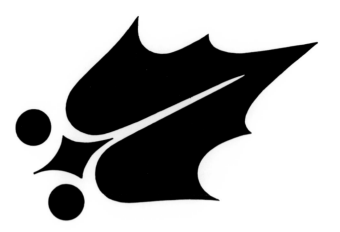

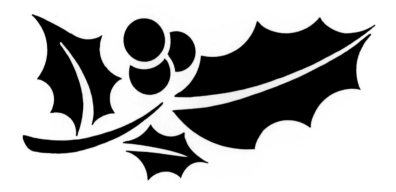

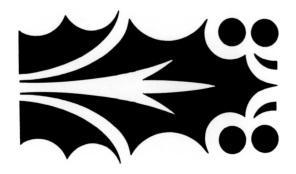

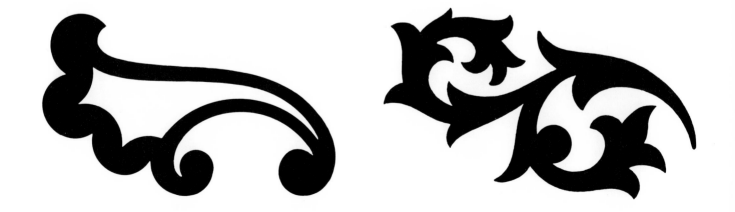

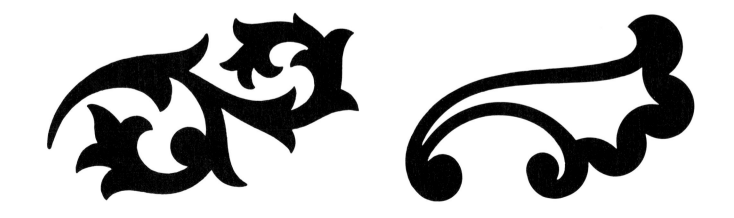

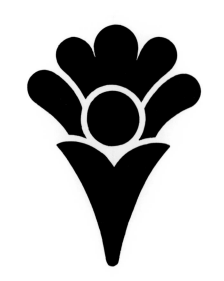

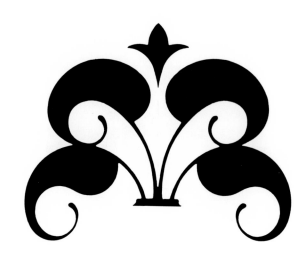

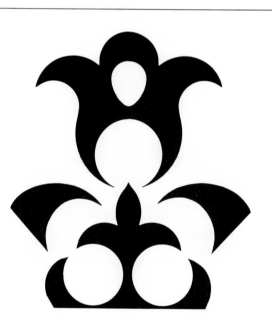

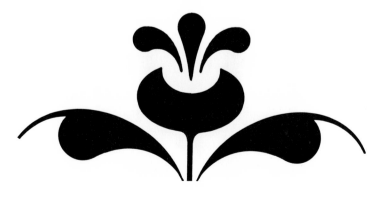

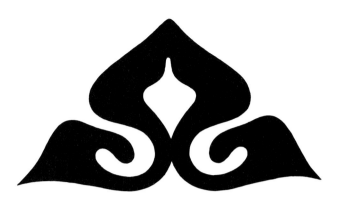

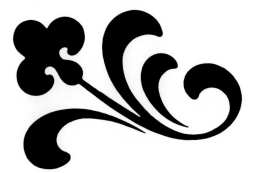

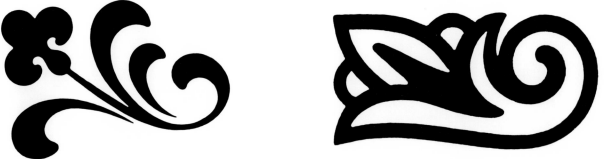

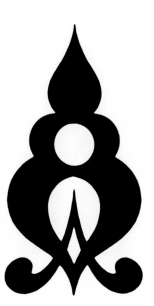

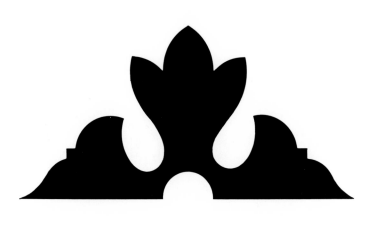

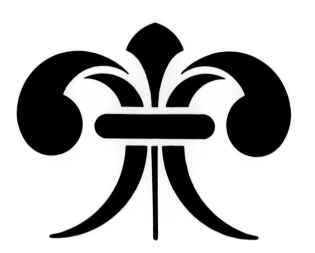
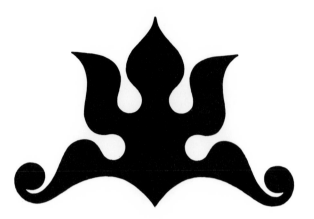

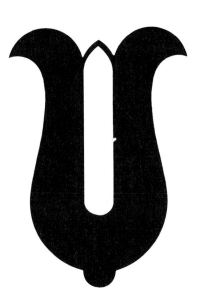

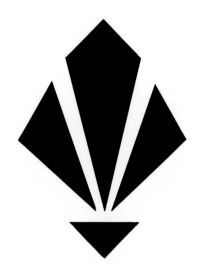

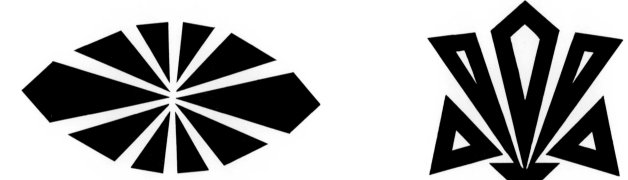

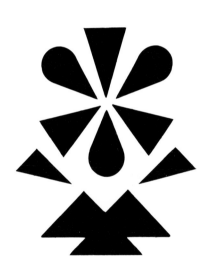

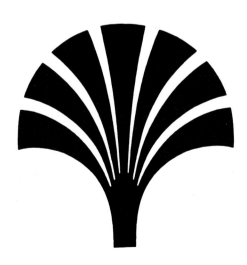

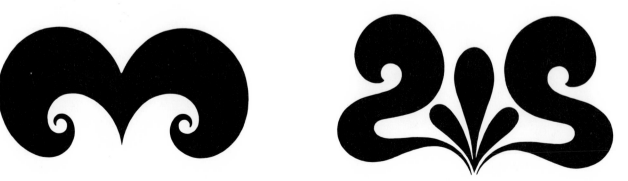

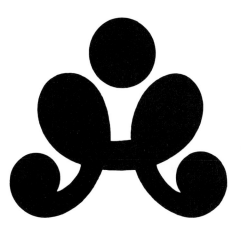

Curvilinear Forms

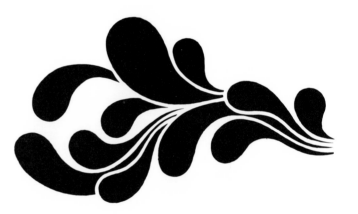

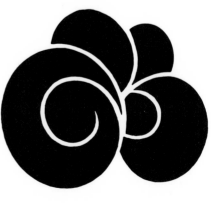

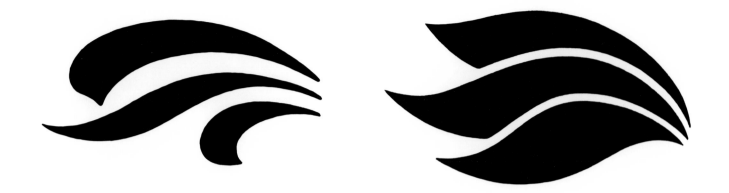

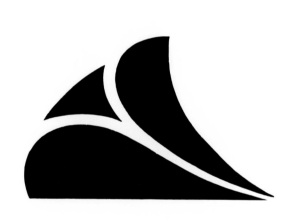

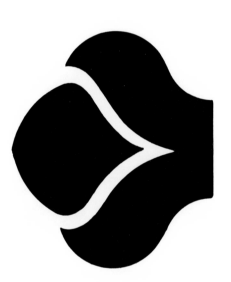

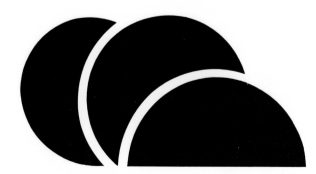

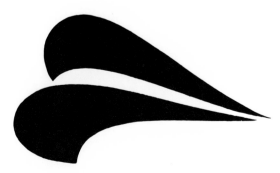

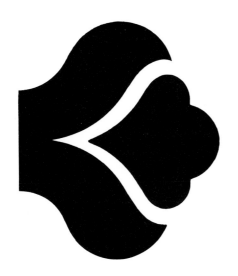

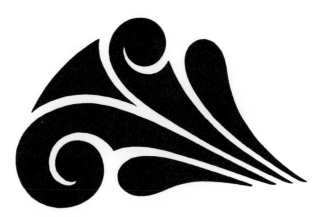

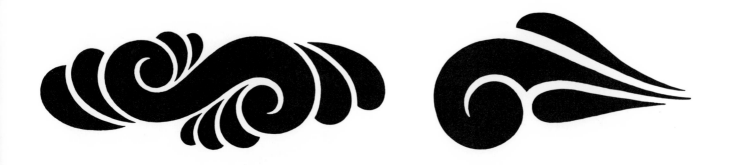

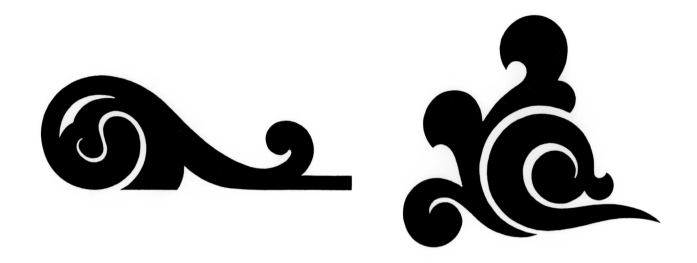

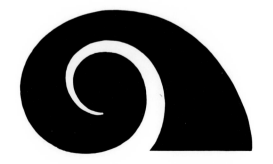

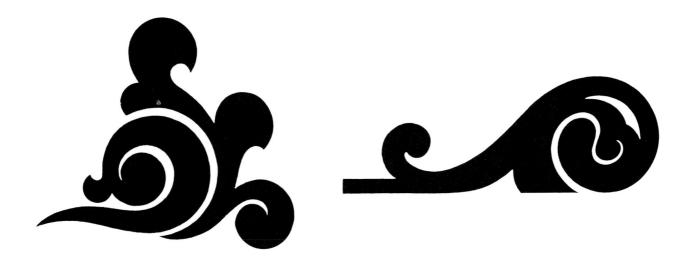

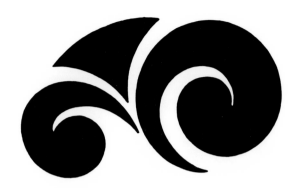

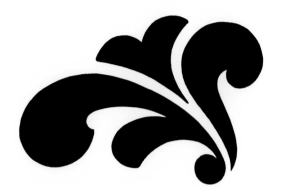

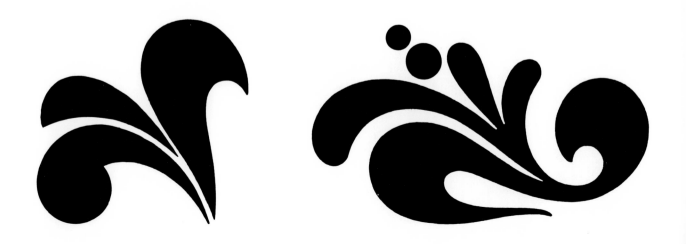

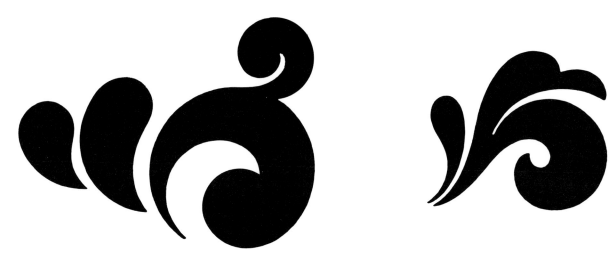

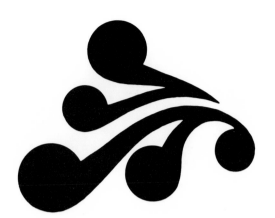
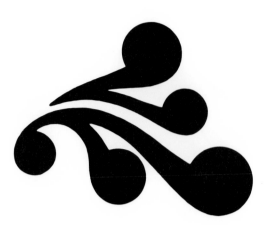

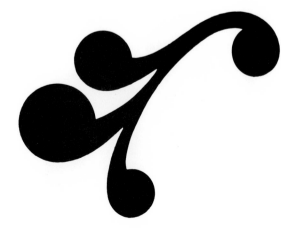

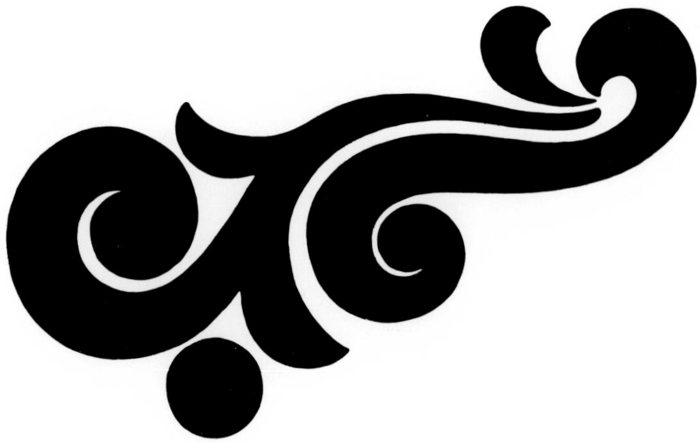

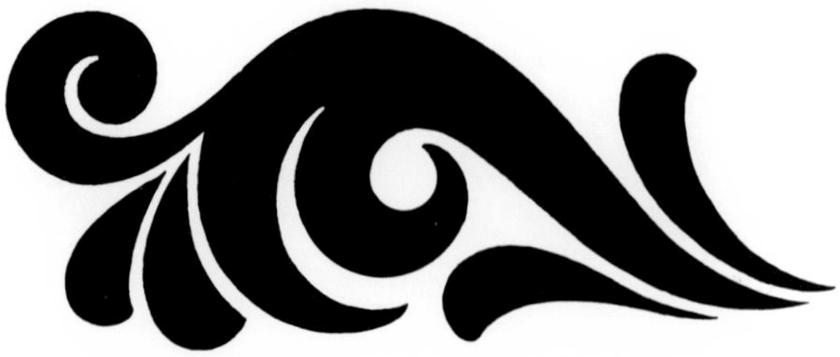

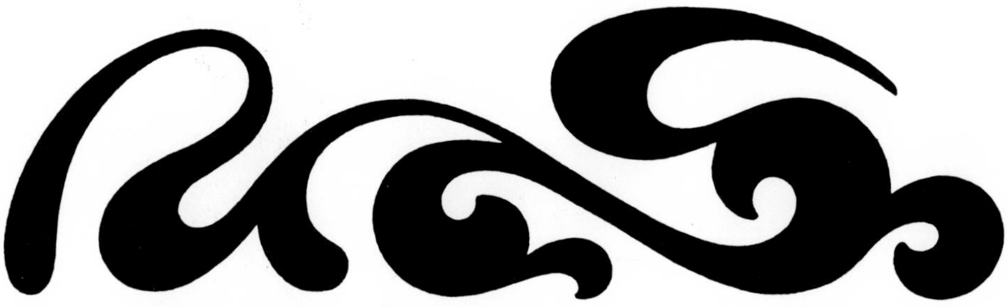

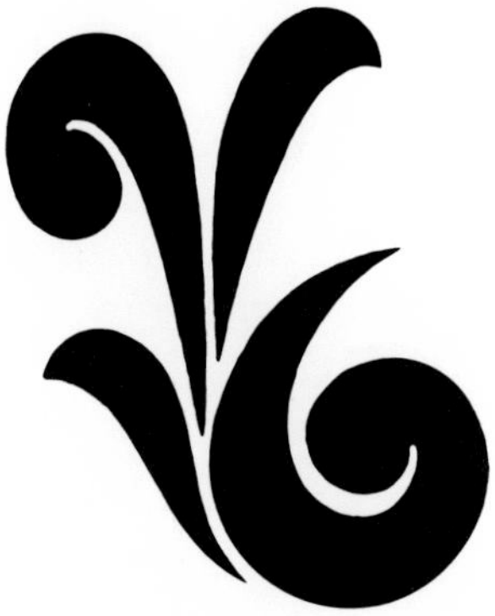

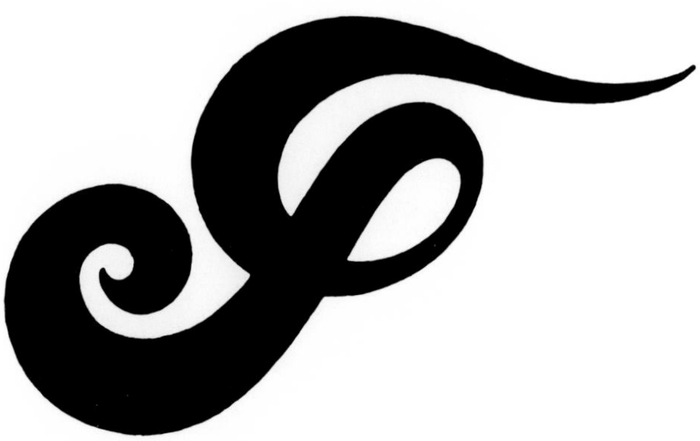

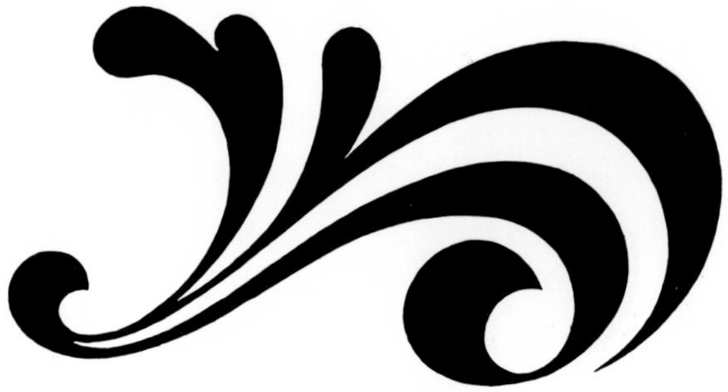

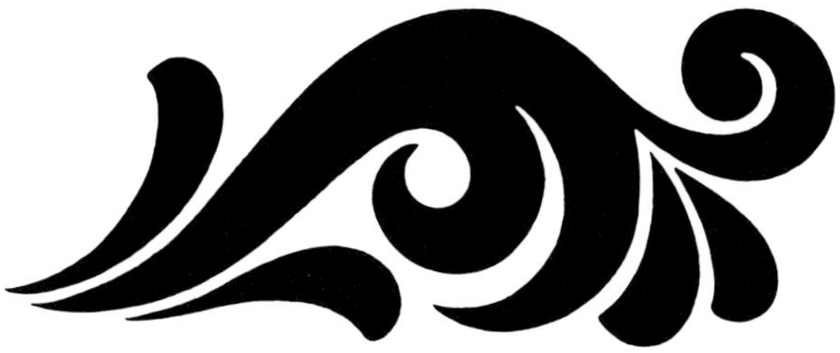

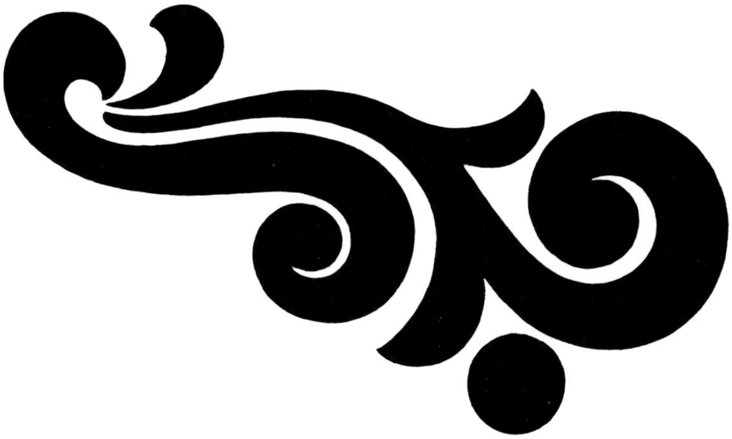

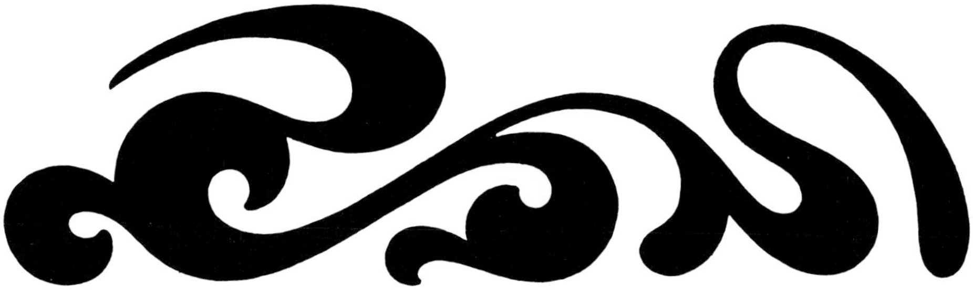

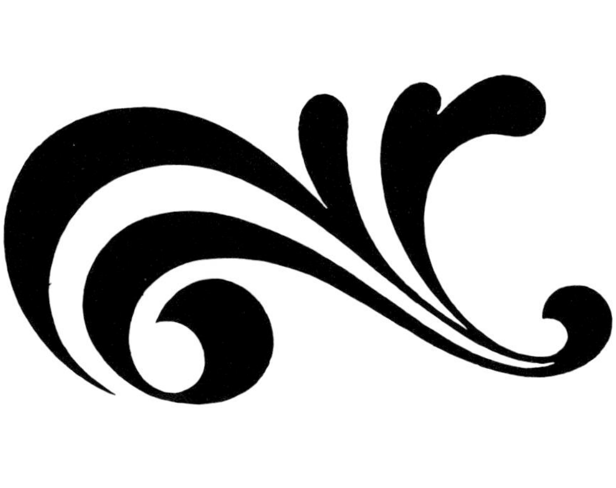

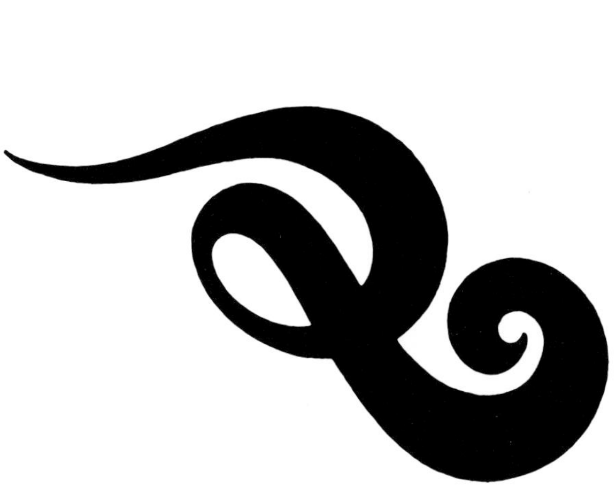

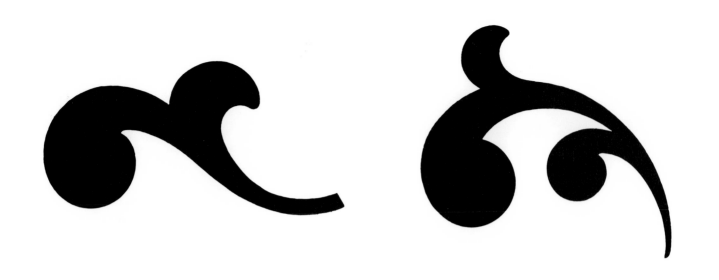

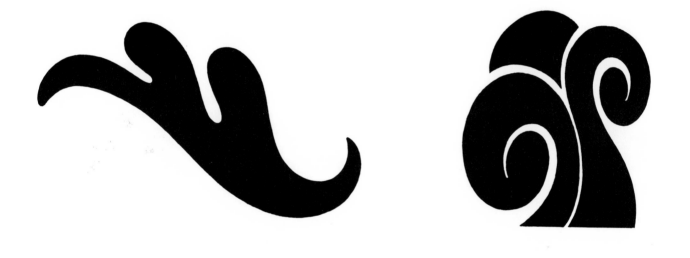

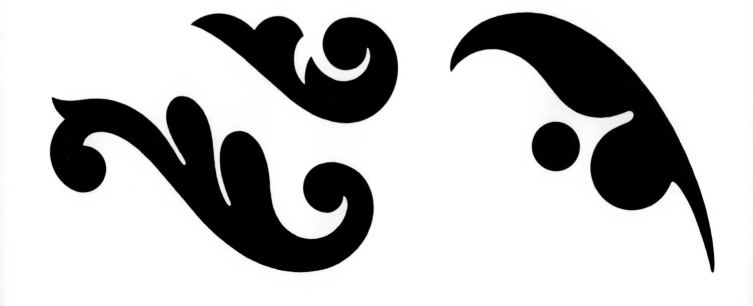

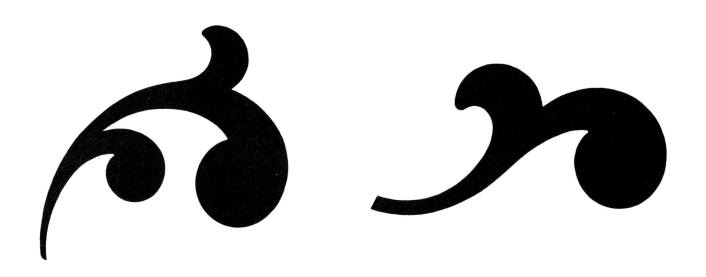

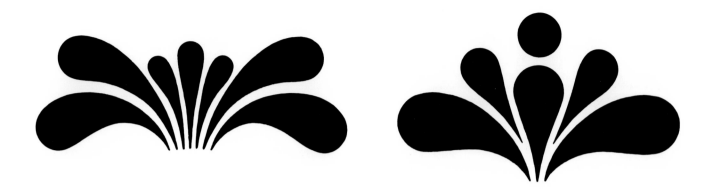

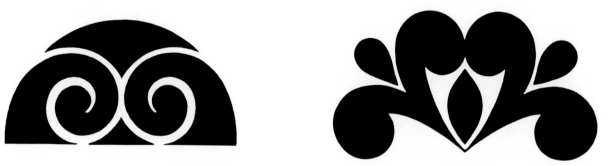

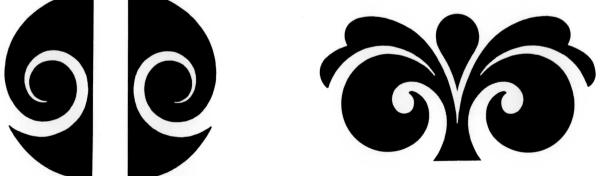

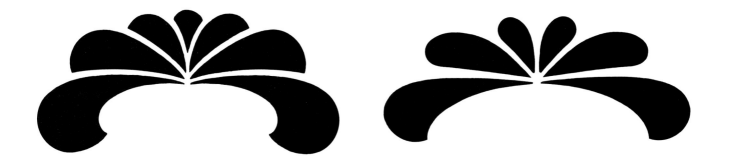

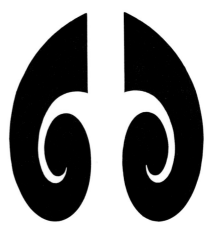

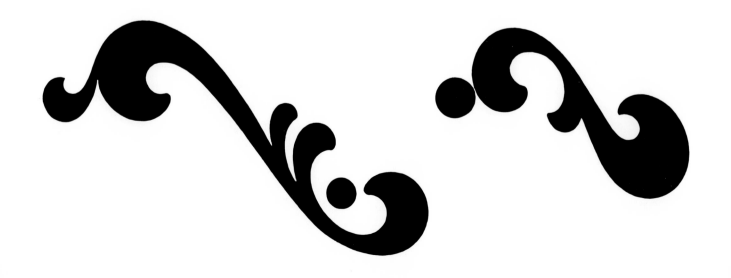

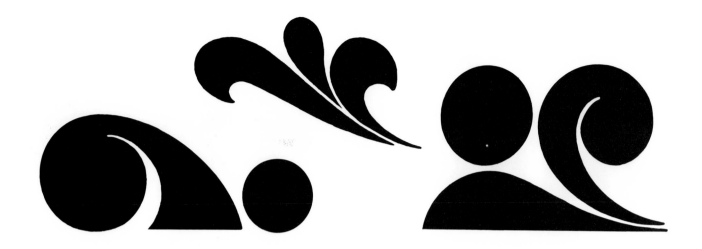

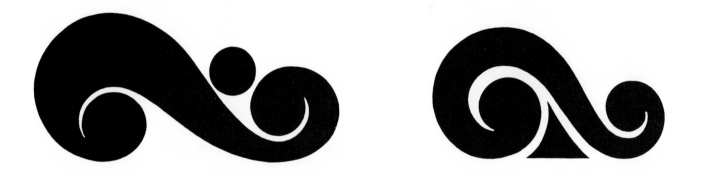

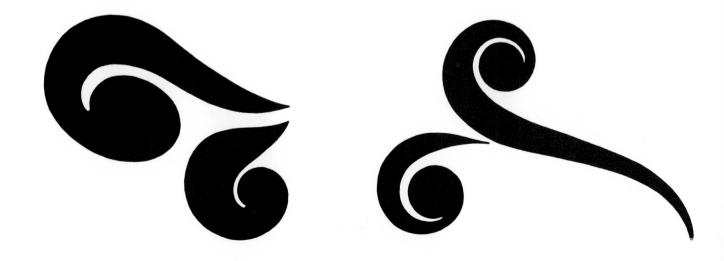

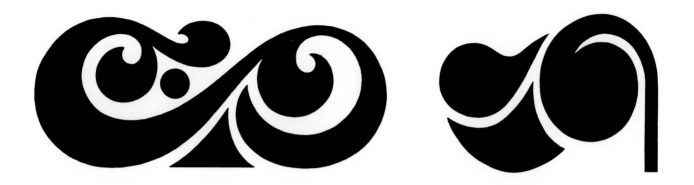

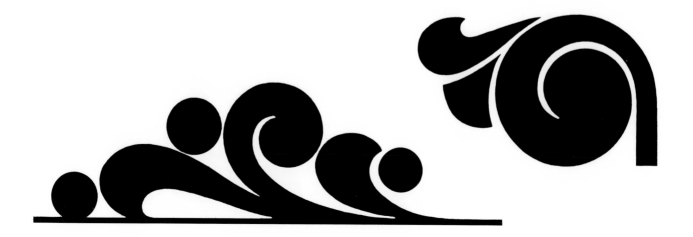

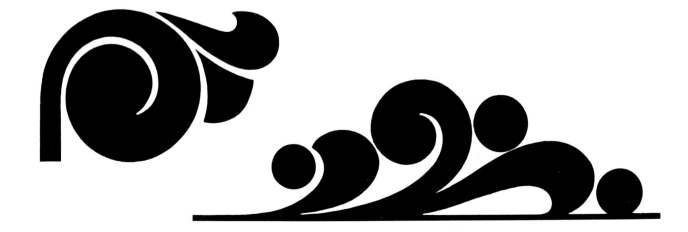

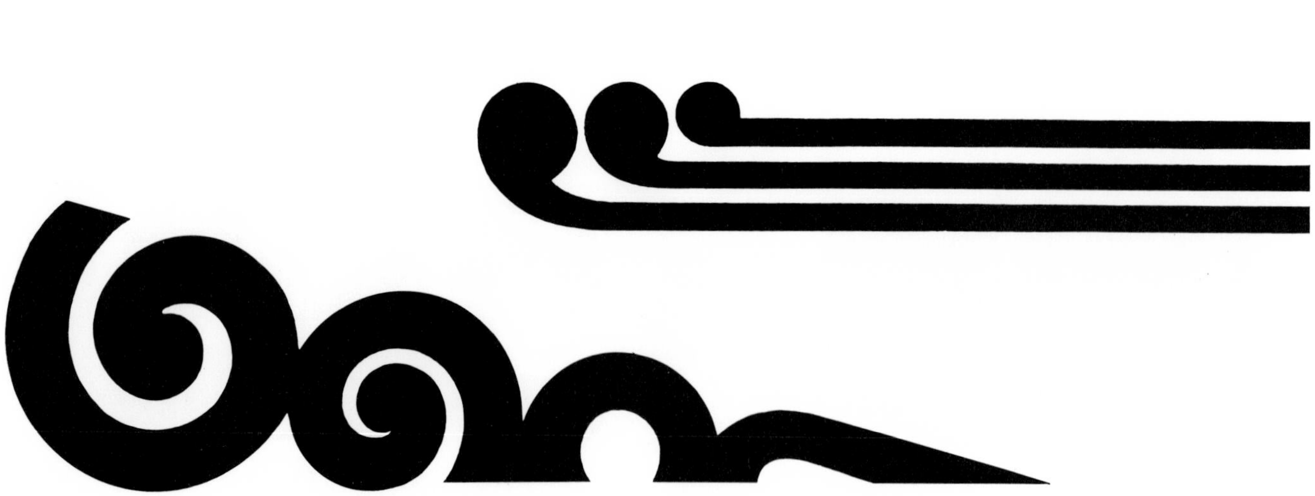

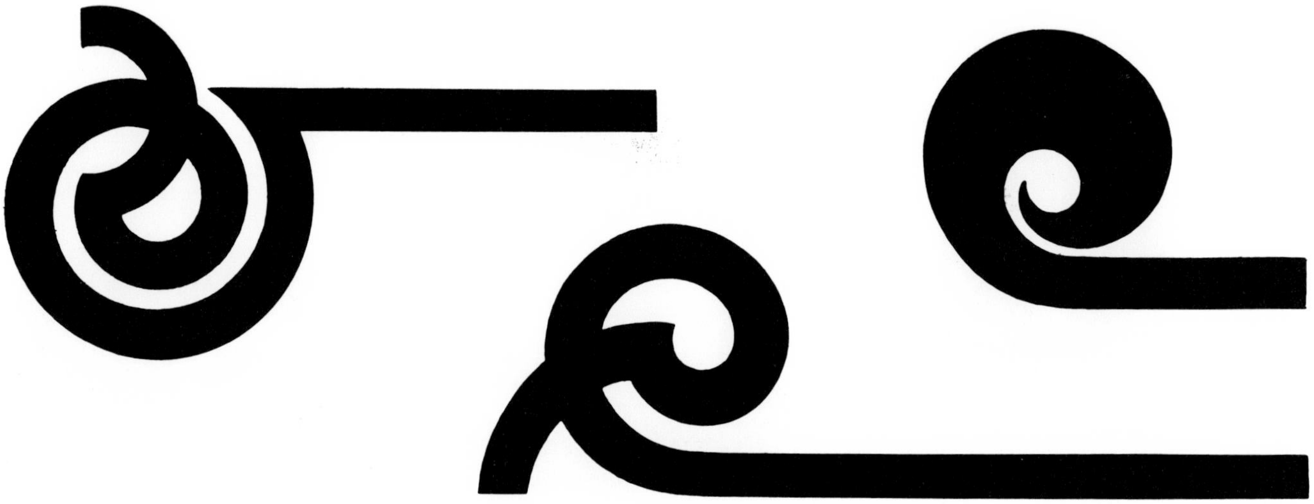

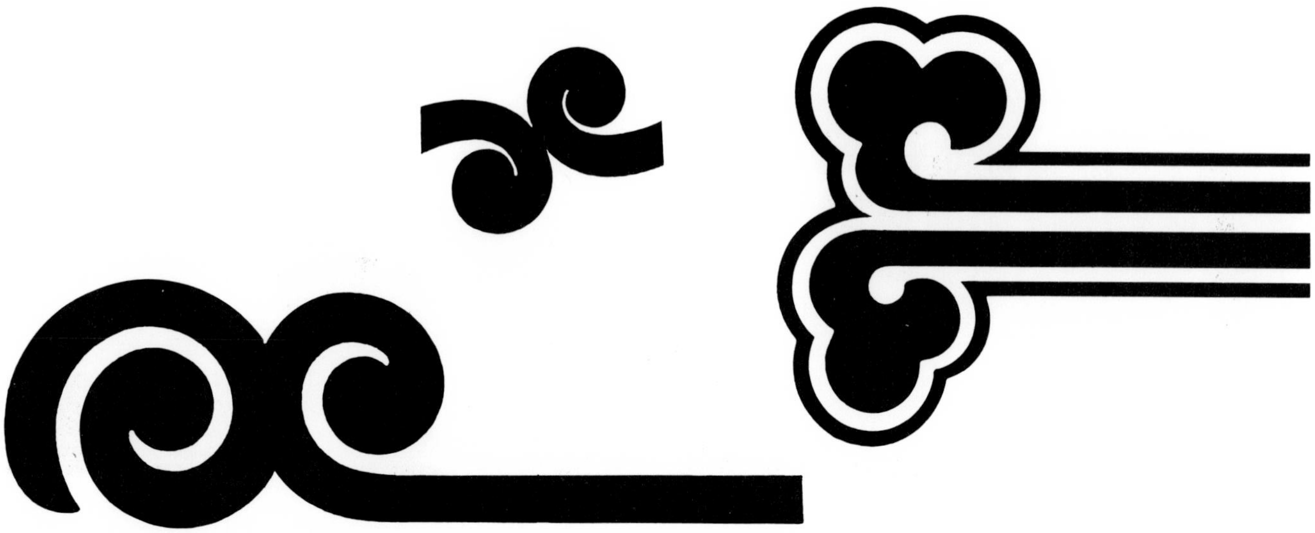

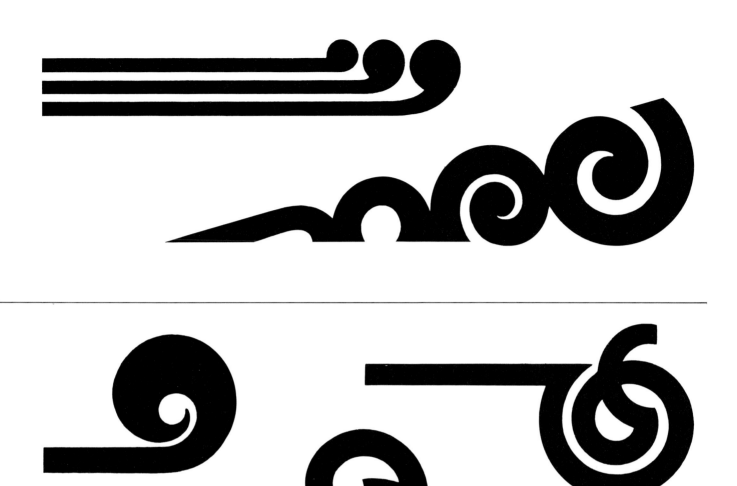

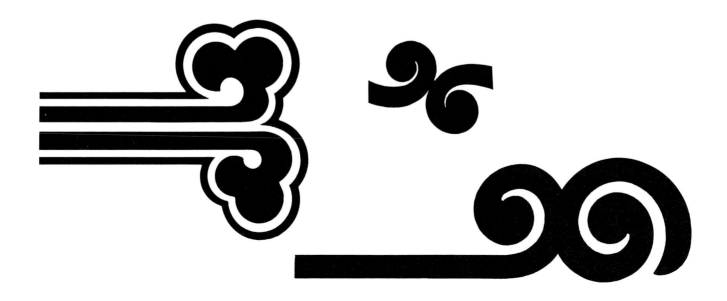

Spencerian Flourishes
Spencerian Accents
Ornamental Frames

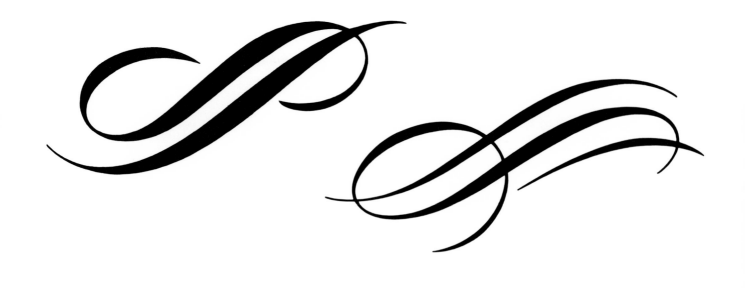

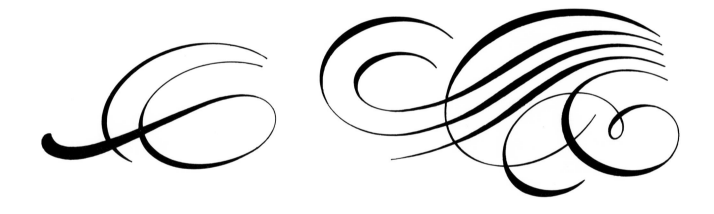

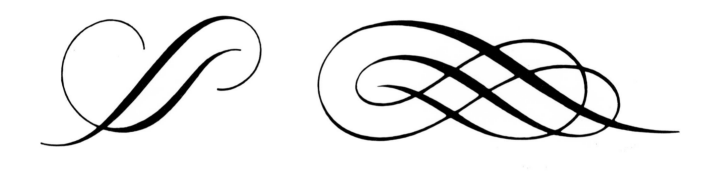

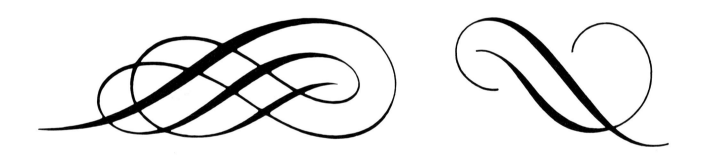

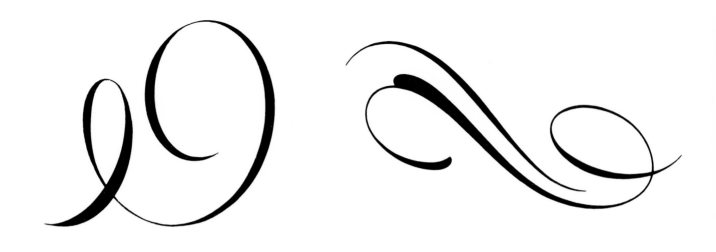

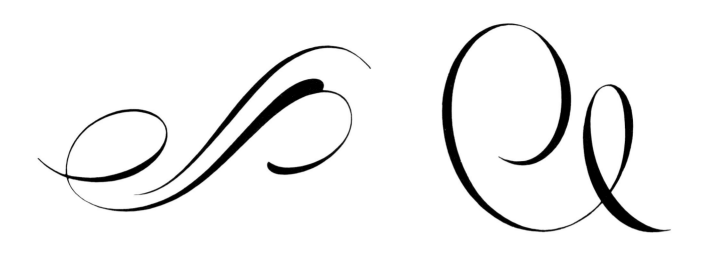

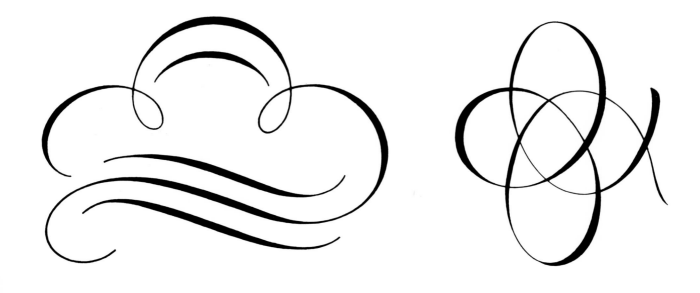

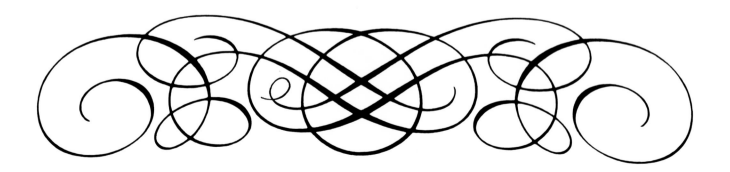

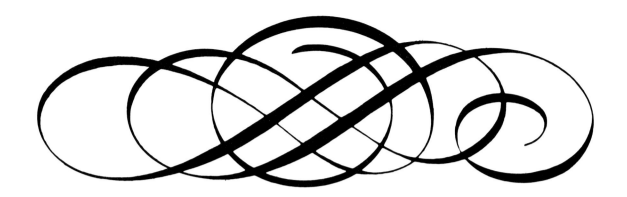

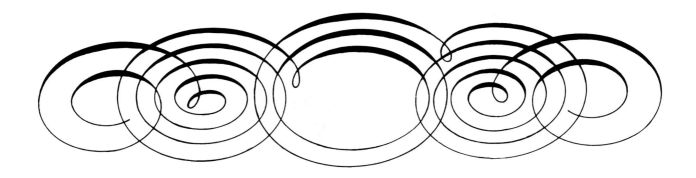

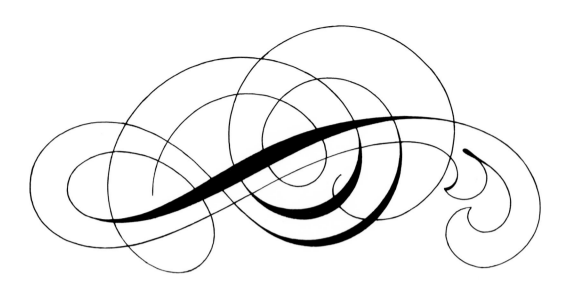

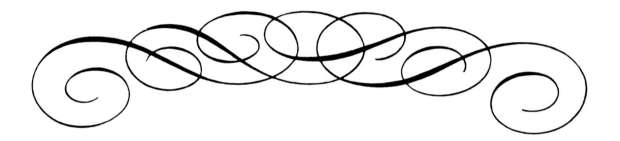

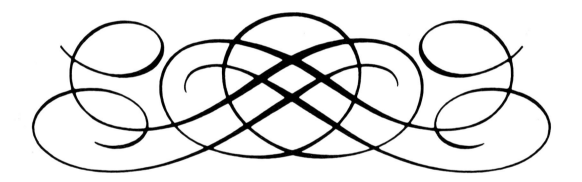

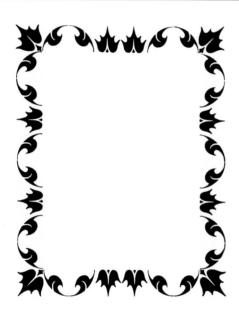

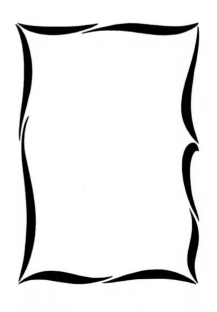

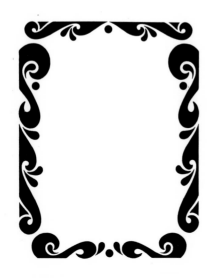